Investigating Manufacturing Pollution

Cynthia Kennedy Henzel

Wonder Books
An Imprint of The Child's World®
childsworld.com

The Child's World
childsworld.com

Published by The Child's World®
800-599-READ • www.childsworld.com

Photography Credits
Photographs ©: Susan Santa Maria/Shutterstock Images, cover, 2; Sved Oliver/Shutterstock Images, 5; DS/AP Images, 6; AP Images, 9; Shutterstock Images, 11, 20, 22, 29, 31; Red Line Editorial, 12; Belovodchenko Anton/Shutterstock Images, 15; Alen Thien/Shutterstock Images, 16; Jamie Hooper/Shutterstock Images, 18; Michael Dechev/Shutterstock Images, 24; M Image Photography/Shutterstock Images, 26

ISBN Information
9781503858107 (Reinforced Library Binding)
9781503860094 (Portable Document Format)
9781503861459 (Online Multi-user eBook)
9781503862814 (Electronic Publication)

LCCN 2021952393

Printed in the United States of America

BRINGING THE WORLD TO YOUNG READERS 1968

ABOUT THE AUTHOR

Cynthia Kennedy Henzel has a bachelor's degree in social studies education and a master's degree in geography. She has written more than 100 books and 150 stories for young people.

Factories often release pollution into the air.

TABLE OF CONTENTS

CHAPTER ONE

DISASTER ZONE

In the 1940s, the Hooker Chemicals and Plastics Corporation bought some land near Niagara Falls, New York. The company needed a place to dump **chemical waste**, so it dug a pit. The company lined the pit with clay. It filled barrels with 22,000 tons (20,000 metric tons) of waste. It put the barrels in the pit. Then Hooker covered the pit with more clay. This area was called Love Canal.

In 1953, Hooker sold the land to the city of Niagara Falls. The city built homes and a school in the area. Soon, hundreds of houses lined the streets.

Barrels of chemical waste can hurt the environment, including the soil, water, and wildlife.

In 1978, people who were affected by the dangerous chemicals from Love Canal's pollution held many protests. The protests made news reporters and the government notice the situation.

But in the 1970s, trees and other plants began to die. Children playing in rain puddles came home with rashes and blisters on their skin. Bicycle tires and children's shoes started to fall apart in puddles of water. During heavy rains, barrels filled with **toxic** chemicals floated to the surface in people's yards.

Love Canal was leaking. Toxic chemicals **polluted** the soil and water. People were getting sick. Some people had lung and heart problems. Some children had learning disabilities. The number of babies born with physical and mental health problems rose.

In 1979, the federal government moved people in the city to safe areas. Congress passed laws to provide money to clean up polluted areas. These areas were called Superfund sites. The government and private companies spent $300 million to clean up Love Canal. The federal government put 3 feet (.9 m) of clay and heavy plastic on top of the site. Drains were built to collect water. The government put in a system to clean the 5 million gallons (19 million L) of toxic water that leaked into playgrounds and people's yards. Groundwater was carefully monitored to make sure no chemicals escaped.

In the 1990s, the U.S. Environmental Protection Agency (EPA) said the site was safe. The EPA is a government agency. It is in charge of protecting the environment. Builders put up new homes. People moved in. But in 2018, some people living near Love Canal noticed bad smells in their homes.

People had terrible headaches. Others had breathing problems. They filed a lawsuit against the government. They thought Love Canal was not as safe as the government had told them.

The Love Canal disaster is one example of **manufacturing** pollution. Manufacturing pollution is when factories or mines release toxic materials into the environment. In 2021, more than 1,000 Superfund sites waited for cleanup. Many of them were close to homes and schools.

Manufacturing pollution can cause serious problems. It makes the land unsafe to live on.

CHAPTER TWO

A CHEMICAL WORLD

Chemicals are everywhere. They are in paint, glue, paper, and ink. Factories use chemicals to make the metal for bicycles. They use chemicals to make clothes, shoes, and jewelry. All plastic is made with chemicals. Chemicals can even keep food fresh and make it taste better.

In the early 1700s, people made most things by hand. This took a long time. In the late 1700s, factories began making goods in Great Britain. This period is called the Industrial Revolution. The Industrial Revolution changed how people lived. The cost of goods became cheaper. So, many people moved from farms to cities. They bought more factory goods.

Many factories use chemicals to make various products.

Making more goods means using more chemicals. Extra chemicals become waste. Factories get rid of waste by dumping it into the water or on the land. This pollutes the environment. Today, factories use thousands of different chemicals to make goods. Manufacturing creates 22 percent of all pollution in the United States.

CHEMICAL WASTE BY INDUSTRY, 2019

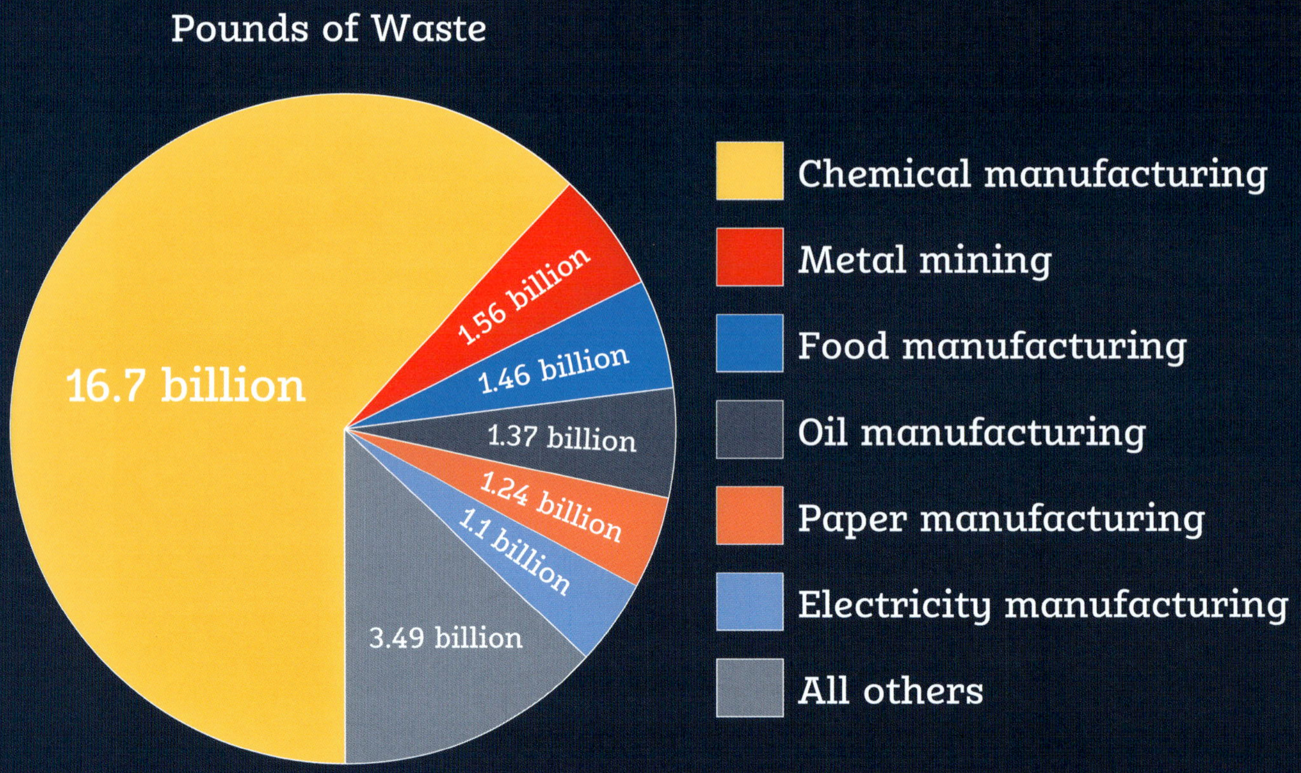

Some types of manufacturing deal with more chemicals than others. In 2019, most chemicals in the United States came from chemical manufacturing.

PFAS

PFAS are a group of chemicals. They are used to make paper, plastic, clothing, carpet, and other goods. They do not break down over time. PFAS build up in the soil and water. They also stay inside plants and the animals that eat the plants. The chemicals can harm people, too. Health problems include cancer and damage to the liver and kidneys. Many PFAS can no longer be used in the United States. But products that come from other countries may still have dangerous PFAS.

One way factories cause pollution is by burning fossil fuels such as coal, oil, or natural gas. When factories burn fossil fuels, lots of carbon dioxide is released into the air. Carbon dioxide is a greenhouse gas. Greenhouse gases trap heat near Earth's surface. They make the planet warmer. Greenhouse gases increased as factories grew. Factories make 23 percent of greenhouse gases in the United States.

A second way that manufacturing produces waste is by using chemical **processes**. This means chemicals are used to make a product. Chemical processes include using paint and polish to make furniture. They also include using bleach and dye to make clothing. For example, when jeans are made, they are dyed a specific shade of blue. Different colors of dye contain a lot of chemicals. It is hard to take the chemicals out of the water that was used to dye the jeans.

A third type of manufacturing pollution is the release of small particles into the air. Some particles are in smoke from burning fossil fuels. The manufacturing of products such as cement makes dust particles. These small particles of smoke and dust can get into people's lungs and cause damage.

CHAPTER THREE

WASHING AWAY WASTE

The easiest way for a factory to get rid of chemical waste is to dump it in a stream or another body of water. The water carries away the chemical waste. Of course, the waste does not disappear. The water takes it to a new place. Seventy percent of all manufacturing pollution in the world is dumped directly into water.

Polluted water affects animals that live there. It also affects people's health. This is because the polluted water can go into drinking water or into crops.

When algae grow rapidly and make the water a different color, it is called an algae bloom.

Many chemicals released by factories are toxic to plants and animals. Water near factories can become very polluted. Sometimes nothing can live in it. Some chemicals cause plants called algae to grow. Algae turn the water green or red. An overgrowth of algae leads to less oxygen in the water. Fish in the water die from too little oxygen.

IT'S HOT!

Thermal pollution is when factories cool or heat water and then release it into the environment. Companies that make paper, metal products, and chemicals use a lot of hot water. Other companies use water to cool hot machines. However, this heats up the water. Thermal pollution can change the oxygen level in the water and kill fish. There are some ways to solve this problem. Factories can fill cooling ponds or towers with their hot water. Then the water can cool before it is released.

Some chemicals build up in plants and animals over time. Mercury is one chemical that stays inside living things. If mercury is in the water, fish can absorb it through their skin. When fish eat plants, they get even more mercury. That is because plants absorb mercury from the water. Small fish eat the plants. Then large fish eat the smaller fish. They get even more mercury in their bodies. People can then eat the fish. If people eat fish with too much mercury, they can get sick.

Heavy metals, including mercury, are toxic in tiny amounts. Heavy metals include arsenic. Arsenic is used to make electronics. Arsenic can cause cancer. Another heavy metal is cadmium. Cadmium is used to make batteries. Cadmium affects the kidneys and bones.

Lead is a heavy metal. People once used it to make water pipes. It was also used in paint. In addition, people used lead in electronics to put pieces together. No amount of lead is safe for people. Lead has been replaced with safer materials in pipes, paint, and electronics. But lead can still be found in tiny amounts in products such as lipstick.

Older buildings often have lead paint. People may need to remove old paint when they move to a new home because the paint can be toxic.

CHAPTER FOUR

DIRTY SOIL

Bacteria and other living things are part of the soil. Heavy metals and chemicals kill living things in the soil. When pollution gets into soil, plants cannot grow there.

Soil helps make water cleaner. Soil particles trap chemicals as water flows through the soil. This is one way soil is polluted. Some soil is polluted from radioactive waste. Radioactive waste comes from nuclear plants that make electricity.

Soil is also polluted when factories dump waste on the land. For example, many manufacturers use oil. Oil can be used to make plastics. Factories use oil to keep equipment working. But oil that is put into the soil stays there.

People use large machines to drill into the ground when searching for metals.

Mining for metals causes soil pollution, too. Metals such as lead, copper, silver, and gold are usually expensive. They are used in jewelry. They are also used to make electronics. Digging for these metals may release heavy metals buried deep in the ground. Some mines use chemicals to separate the metals from the rock. The wastewater from this process is very polluted. It must be kept in ponds that will not leak.

Polluted soil is very difficult to clean. Sometimes, engineers remove the soil and replace it with new soil. They may wash the soil they remove to get rid of toxins. This is expensive. Large grains of soil can be washed and used again. But engineers must safely dispose of the water, toxins, and fine particles of soil. New methods to clean soil use plants. Some plants absorb toxic material as they grow. The plants can then be cut down and destroyed or stored in a safe place. Soil that cannot be cleaned must be stored somewhere safe.

SMARTPHONES AND POLLUTION

Smartphones are everywhere. People want new smartphones every few years. But the process to make smartphones creates a lot of pollution. The process uses a lot of water. It also uses expensive heavy metals and other toxic chemicals. Most smartphone parts are made in countries that do not have strict environmental laws.

To see if soil is polluted, people can sample the area. They test the soil in a laboratory.

Today, the EPA has strict laws on where factories can dump waste. Dangerous waste must be put into safe containers. However, some factories still dump waste. They do not want to pay to make waste safe. If they are caught, they have to pay large fines. Sometimes the factory owners go to jail.

The EPA keeps an eye on mines in the United States, too. Most of the waste is kept at the mining site. But other countries often have laws that are less strict.

CHAPTER FIVE

CLEAN MANUFACTURING

In the early 1900s, factories in the United States grew quickly. There were no laws about how to get rid of waste. Factories dumped waste everywhere. By the 1960s, the air, water, and soil were very polluted. Nothing could live in parts of the Great Lakes because of pollution. Air pollution in cities caused hundreds of deaths each year. The Cuyahoga River in Cleveland, Ohio, caught fire because factories had dumped so much oil into the water.

Companies can clean their contaminated water in wastewater treatment plants.

Factories cannot make products without making waste. But today the EPA makes sure that factories in the United States treat waste properly. Factories must get permission from the EPA to release waste into waterways. The EPA makes sure the waste is safe.

The EPA also cleans up areas that are already polluted. It has spent billions of dollars to clean waterways. Still, more than half of the nation's streams have poor **ecosystems** because of pollution.

The news is not all bad. Manufacturing pollution has decreased in many wealthy countries. Today, factories use less energy. They also use more clean energy. That means companies use new processes that make less pollution.

RECYCLED JEANS

The fashion industry creates a lot of pollution when making products. Some fashion companies have made efforts to reduce their waste. Levi's is a popular clothing company. It has created a new process that uses 96 percent less water to make a pair of jeans. Levi's has also started making jeans out of recycled plastic bottles.

Scientists and engineers have found cheaper ways to recycle toxic chemicals and heavy metals. For example, **microbes** that clean water can be used in industrial processes. Also, more factories are treating their wastewater so that the water can be reused. The treatment can help take out toxic heavy metals or chemicals.

When buying clothes, people can be more aware about where a product was manufactured.

Many people who are affected by manufacturing pollution live in poorer countries. This is because a lot of big companies manufacture their goods in poorer countries. Land, electricity, and labor are cheaper there. However, this is all at the cost of workers' health. The land also suffers. Some governments are working to create better rules for factories. But a lot of work still needs to be done.

Consumers are people who buy goods. Most people are consumers. Therefore, consumers can be a big help in reducing manufacturing pollution.

Consumers can learn how companies manufacture their goods. Then they can choose to buy or not buy certain products. For example, they can buy clothing from a company that uses clean energy instead of fossil fuels. Consumers can also check if the company pays its workers fairly.

People can also ask their governments to give more money to clean up pollution. The Superfund Act of 1980 was possible because the U.S. government taxed chemical and oil companies. In addition, people can ask their governments not to buy goods made in countries that pollute the environment. Many wealthy countries have a lot less manufacturing pollution than 50 years ago. New technology and laws can help reduce it even more.

FAST FACTS

- Manufacturing is a major source of pollution for air, water, and soil.
- Air pollution created by manufacturing is mainly produced through burning fossil fuels.
- Factories pollute water by dumping waste chemicals into bodies of water. This can cause the water to be unusable by people, plants, and animals.
- Soil pollution happens when factories dump waste. Other soil pollution from factories happens when chemicals escape into the soil from polluted water.
- Heavy metals are dangerous manufacturing chemicals. They can build up in plants, the animals that eat the plants, and people.
- The U.S. Environmental Protection Agency is responsible for keeping track of manufacturing pollution. It also cleans up areas that are dangerously polluted.
- People can help decrease manufacturing pollution. They can use fewer manufactured products and waste fewer goods.

HOW SOIL HOLDS WATER

MATERIALS

- 1 coffee filter
- Funnel
- Beaker
- 1 cup of soil
- Measuring cup
- Water

DIRECTIONS

1. Place the coffee filter into the funnel. Then place the funnel into the beaker.
2. Put 1 cup of soil into the filter.
3. Pour 1/4 cup (60 mL) of water onto the soil.
4. Wait for two minutes.
5. Take out the funnel. Pour the water inside the beaker into a measuring cup.
6. How much water moved through the soil into the beaker? What does this tell you about how much polluted water soil might be able to hold?

GLOSSARY

chemical waste (KEM-ih-kuhl WAYST) Chemical waste is leftover chemicals that factories need to dispose of. The water's bad smell is because of chemical waste.

ecosystems (EE-koh-siss-tuhms) Ecosystems are all the living things that work together in their environments. Pollution destroyed the ecosystems by killing the plants.

manufacturing (man-yoo-FAK-chur-ing) Manufacturing is the process of making something with machines. Manufacturing pollution can hurt the environment.

microbes (MYE-krobes) Microbes are very small organisms that can cause sickness or can be good for people's health. Some microbes can clean water.

polluted (puh-LOO-ted) Polluted means to have added waste to the environment. The air was polluted with smoke from the factory.

processes (PRAH-ses-es) Processes are the steps to do something. Companies use chemical processes to make products.

toxic (TAHK-sik) Toxic means something is harmful or poisonous. The smoke from the factory was toxic.

WAYS YOU CAN HELP

- Avoid wasting products that are manufactured, such as paper, plastic, and electronics.
- Identify Superfund sites near you. Write letters to your members of Congress about cleaning up Superfund sites.
- Research companies that are doing things to reduce pollution. Learn about what they are doing. Then research a company that does not work to reduce pollution. Write a letter to that company with helpful ideas on how to reduce pollution.

FIND OUT MORE

In the Library

Furgang, Kathy. *Clean Water and Our Future*. New York, NY: PowerKids Press, 2022.

Hustad, Douglas. *How Can We Reduce Manufacturing Pollution?* Minneapolis, MN: Lerner, 2016.

Perdew, Laura. *Investigating Plastic Pollution*. Mankato, MN: The Child's World, 2023.

On the Web

Visit our website for links about investigating manufacturing pollution: **childsworld.com/links**

Note to Parents, Teachers, and Librarians: We routinely verify our Web links to make sure they are safe and active sites. So encourage your readers to check them out!

INDEX